Old WARRENPOINT & ROSTREVOR

by
Alex F. Young, with photographs from the Tommy O'Hanlon

The Esplanade, photographed from an upper window of the Great Northern Hotel in 1911. A horse-drawn tram is passing the swimming pool. Within fifteen months of the town council's decision to build a swimming pool, as part of their ongoing facility improvement programme, and commissioning the engineers Kaye, Parry & Ross to produce plans, the foundation stone was laid by Mrs Roger Hall in the summer of 1906. The building contract was awarded to H. & J. Martin of Dublin, but was soon beset with problems. Working in tidal water necessitated a night shift, which threatened a strike amongst the workers until they were offered an hourly rate above the day shift's. The tides also brought structural movement until buttresses were installed. However, from the opening, on Monday 8 June 1908, the baths were a success, showing a profit of £322 in the first year, and having 55,127 visitors in its first full season in 1909.

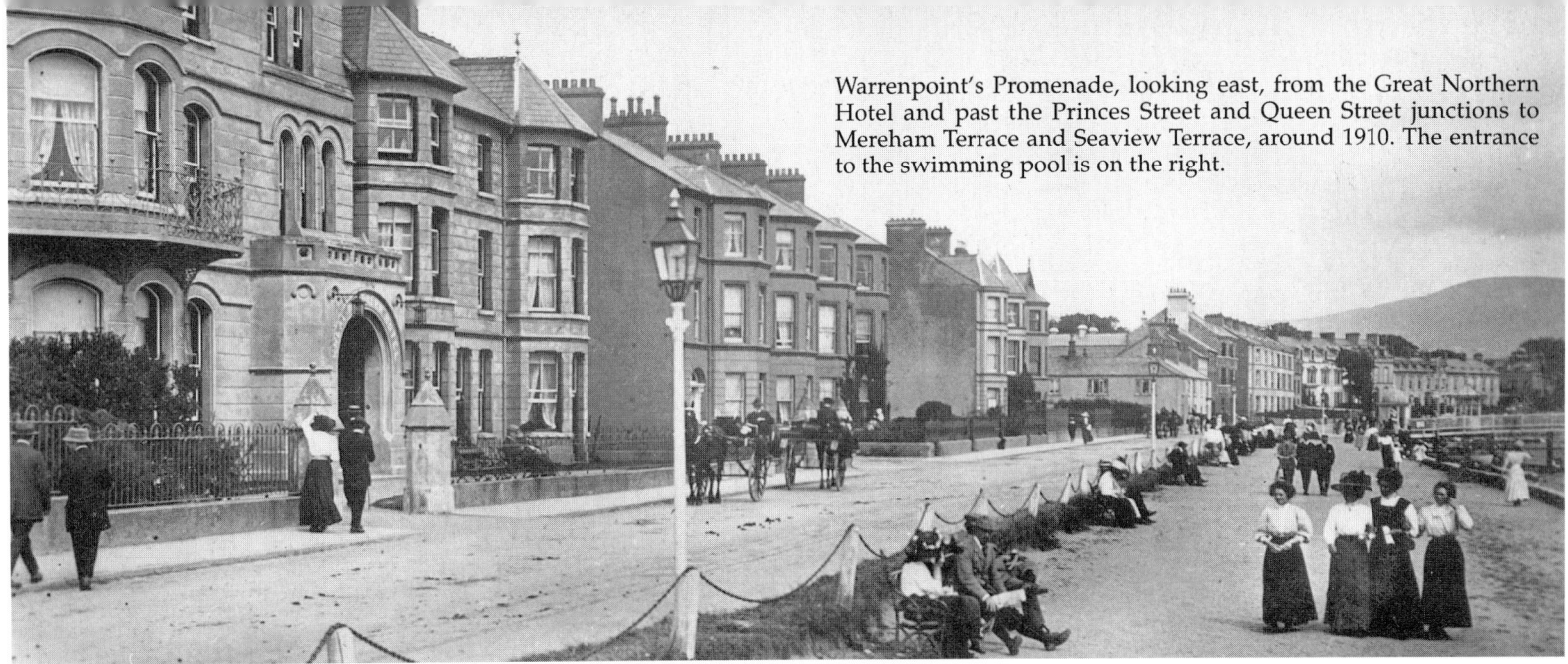

Warrenpoint's Promenade, looking east, from the Great Northern Hotel and past the Princes Street and Queen Street junctions to Mereham Terrace and Seaview Terrace, around 1910. The entrance to the swimming pool is on the right.

FURTHER READING

The books listed below were used by the author during his research. Only one is available from Stenlake Publishing Ltd. Those interested in finding out more are advised to contact their local bookshop or reference library.

Angelique Day and Patrick McWilliams, *Ordnance Survey Memoirs of Ireland: Parishes of County Down 1, 1834–6, South Down*, The Institute of Irish Studies, Queen's University of Belfast.
W. Haughton Crowe, *Village in Seven Hills*, 1972.
Stephen Johnson, *Lost Railways of Co. Down and Co. Armagh*, Stenlake Publishing, 2002.
James Kilroy, *Irish Trams*, Colourpoint Press, 1996.
Tom McAteer, *Warrenpoint Golf Club, 1893–1993: A History*, 1993.

ACKNOWLEDGEMENTS

The author wishes to thank for their assistance during his research: Bryan Boyle, Kathleen Brunker, Mary Cahill, Gerard Cowan, Oliver Dinsmore, Marion Eccles, Kieran Fegan, Patricia Gordon, Kevin Hanna, Oliver Havern, Steven Gilmore, Graeme Lorimer, Jim McCart, John McKenna, Michelle McManus, Frank O'Hare, Jim O'Neil, John Joe Parr, Willie Sloan, Wendy Walker, Harry Smith of the Christian Renewal Centre, Florence Fagan of St Joseph's Nursing Home, Warrenpoint Orange Lodge, Jason Diamond of Banbridge Genealogy Services, The Bluecoat Press of Liverpool, Warrenpoint Golf Club, the SELB libraries at Warrenpoint and Newry.

Text © Alex F. Young, 2003.
First published in the United Kingdom, 2003,
by Stenlake Publishing,
Telephone/Fax: 01290 551122
Printed by Cordfall Ltd, Glasgow, G21 2QA

ISBN 1 84033 279 4

The publishers regret that they cannot supply copies of any pictures featured in this book.

Opposite: The Glenmore Hotel, on Rostrevor's Victoria Terrace, about 1913. It is thought to have been built in the late nineteenth century by Francis Charles Needham, third Earl of Kilmorey (1842–1915); the house in the middle distance was for his mother-in-law, Mrs Elizabeth Baldock. It cannot be clearly ascertained over what period the Glenmore was a hotel, but since August 1974 it has been the Christian Renewal Centre.

INTRODUCTION

Warrenpoint

On the south-west coast of County Down, where the Newry River becomes Carlingford Lough, Warrenpoint was established in the eighteenth century, or earlier, with a few seasonally occupied oyster fishermen's huts amongst the hillocks of rabbit warrens. Around 1780, with the building of two stone houses, a settlement was starting and the rabbits were in trouble. However, they were not forgotten – the town taking its name from their former homes – and when the newly formed Town Council took over from the Town Commissioners in 1899, they adopted as the town's crest a seashell, two rabbits and shamrocks.

Between 1780 and J.H. Williams's *Ordnance Survey Memoir* visit in October 1836, seven three-storey houses, 181 two-storey houses, ten one-storey houses and ten thatched cabins – a total of 208 houses – had been erected. A harbour, taking advantage of the sheltered bay in which the town stood, also had a commodious dock. Williams's survey also reported that port dues, based on 1½d per registered ton, brought in about £300, i.e. 48,000 tons. Larger draught vessels, unable to reach Newry, were handled here also. In the famine years of the 1840s, many families left here for America via Liverpool.

The opening of the railway line from Newry in 1849 transformed Warrenpoint into a popular seaside resort and by the early twentieth century three quarters of the townspeople earned their livelihood from visitors. For example, on Friday, 15 August 1902, 2,000 visitors came by rail and to meet this almost overwhelming demand for amenities the Council formed an Amusements Committee which inaugurated the swimming baths, the open air stage on the Promenade, the roller skating rink and the municipal garden with its bandstand.

Whilst the harbour at Newry is now a memory, Warrenpoint Harbour, thanks to its deeper water, has not only survived but grown and prospered. The *Ordnance Survey Memoirs* described it as 'a good commodious dock' built around 1780 by Savage Hall of Narrow Water (who may have received public assistance of £500 towards costs). In 1919 it was sold to John Kelly of Belfast for £16,000 – and in 1971 sold on to Warrenpoint Harbour Authority for £369,000. The modern port, created from an investment of £6.7 million, now handles around two and a half million tons of cargo per annum.

Warrenpoint's days as a resort are over and the thousands who flocked to it by rail during the summers of the early twentieth century are but a memory, the railway station having closed in January 1965. However, unlike other once popular resorts with their empty and dilapidated buildings, the 'point still wears its mantle of prosperity.

Rostrevor

Originally 'Carrickavraghad', Rostrevor started as a community around the estate and castle of the Trevors, Viscounts Dungannon, and became 'Rose-trevor' when Sir Edward Trevor married Rose, only daughter and heiress of Sir Marmaduke Whitchurch, in 1613. When the Ross family bought the Trevor estate around 1690, it was, for a time, known as 'Rosstrevor' before taking the modern spelling.

Records of its early history are scant, but by the 1830s the village had a church, a Roman Catholic chapel, an hotel, four schools and ninety-three two-storey houses and twenty-nine cabins around Church Street, Bridge Street and Back Lane. Only in the late twentieth century did it really expand.

When John Martin built the Quay of Rostrevor in the 1740s, another, almost divorced community developed, which had six houses and nine cabins by the 1830s. It also had a grocer and a spirit dealer serving the small workforce which was employed by James Reilly at his salt works. In the late nineteenth century, it was around the quay that the new Rostrevor, 'an old English village set in a Norwegian fjord', began to develop as 'the fashionable resort for the gentry of both Ulster and Leinster'. Following the building of the Woodside Hotel came the roller skating rink in 1875 (destroyed by fire in 1903) and Norton & Shaw's Mourne Hotel in 1877, which coincided with the opening of the horse-drawn tramway from Warrenpoint.

Today, the large hotels are gone – the premises of motor dealer J.F. Campbell now occupy their site – and although fewer postcards are sent from Rostrevor these days, like Warrenpoint, the village still appears prosperous.

The east side of Warrenpoint's Square, between Church Street and the Crown Hotel on Post Office Street (now Mary Street) corner, was dominated by the Windmill. According to the *Ordnance Survey Memoirs*, it was built by Robert Turner in 1802 and produced oats; by 1835 it was in the hands of Messrs Isaac William Glenny & Sons. However, according to the *Dublin Penny Journal* of 23 August 1834, it was built before 1760, and was known as 'The Manor Mill', later becoming 'Turner's'. Of its estimated height of ninety feet, some thirty feet of the base remains. The chimney to its left served the furnace which powered a sixteen horsepower steam engine which was used when there was no wind.

The Square, or Dock Square as it was once known, photographed on a market or fair day around 1906, with Charlotte Street and Duke Street in the background. Markets were held each Friday – the last in each month being a fair. Market days were for general trade – yarn, grain, meat, fish, pigs, poultry and eggs – whilst fairs were for cattle and sheep.

Another early twentieth century fair day stretched across the Square, with a funfair, perhaps Toft & Turnbull's, by the Charlotte Street corner. Following a Town Council decision in 1904 to withhold permission, it may have been there illegally. At some point the ruling was rescinded, for the funfair now makes three visit per year – St Patrick's Day, Easter, and two weeks in August. Of the buildings on the far left side of the Square, Thomas Sturgeon's Ulster Hotel on the corner of Newry Street stands out.

Duke Street, viewed from the Square around 1905. The Post Office is on the left, while on the right are Richard McGuffin's boot and shoe warehouse (now Office Furniture) and Hourican's public house. At that time, Dromore Road, beyond, ran out of town through pastures, although these have now been taken up by Mourne Drive, Iveagh Avenue and St Peter's Primary School.

The predominately residential Summer Hill, looking towards East Street and the arched windowed Masonic Hall in Duke Street. Founded in 1789, St John's Masonic Lodge No. 697, like many early lodges, had a number of venues before purchasing a building, the hall on Duke Street being hired on a 999 year lease from the Hall Estate around 1895. Originally built as a Free Methodist Church, it was also used by the Presbyterian Church before the completion of their new building in Meeting House Street.

This is the hall of Loyal Orange Lodge No. 210 on Great George Street North, photographed shortly after its official opening by Captain James Craig, the Unionist MP for East Down, on Saturday 22 September 1906. Previously, meetings had been held in a cottage on the Dromore Road. In the mid 1990s, Lodge No. 210 amalgamated with Warrenpoint's other Orange lodge, No. 27, but, with the loss of their archives some years ago, much of their early history has vanished.

The newsagent J.C. Ingram and staff outside his shop in Church Street, Warrenpoint, around 1908. Recognising the growing popularity of the bicycle, and the business potential in offering them for hire over the summer, put newspapers and fancy goods into second place. Warrenpoint's two other cycle agents were James Nesbitt, also in Church Street, and E.J. McNeill in Newry Street. Ingram's cycle business went on for another generation, but the advertising board for Carburine Motor Spirit pointed to the future. This photograph comes from a postcard which was sold in the shop.

Church Street from the corner of the Square, with Edward Pedlow's 'Paris House' (now the First Trust Bank) on the right. Pedlow stocked 'millinery in all the latest styles', ladies and children's underclothing and gentlemen's shirts, collars, ties and hats. The line of shops on the left contained the Star Bar, Mrs Cunningham the hardware dealer, and William McGuffin's boot and shoe warehouse – 'repairs neatly executed' – whilst on the right Ingram's cycle wheel literally stands out.

Early twentieth century Charlotte Street, looking to Meeting Street, with Ward Bros. the butchers on the right. In the background is Warrenpoint Presbyterian Church on Meeting Street. In his *Ordnance Survey Memoir* of October 1836, J.H. Williams described this church as 'the new Presbyterian meeting house [hence Meeting Street] of Warrenpoint, situated at the north-western end of a new street [the continuation of Church Street] . . . . It was built in the year 1834 at an expense of 750 [pounds] . . . . It can accommodate 650 persons, the total congregation being 456 and average attendance for nine months being 210, and during the remaining three months [the bathing season] 500.' It is still in use today.

A corner of the Square on a quiet market day with a pen of sheep and a few stalls. The shops in the Square, from the left, were: Foster, Pedlow Bros., and Newell, all drapers; Morgan the grocer; the painter W.J. Coburn; and the Crown Hotel. That Newell, with branches in Dublin and Belfast, had come to Warrenpoint was considered recognition of the town's growing popularity as a resort. The white painted house (centre) was on the far corner of Post Office Street (now Mary Street) and the start of South Quay (now Dock Street).

The South Quay, coming from the left and turning into Marine Parade. The old Dutch style roofed Harbour Master's building (long since gone) is to the right. The provision merchant on the corner is R.L. Robinson, later Parkinson & Co. and later again Moffit's. Berthed at the quay is the ninety foot schooner *Nellie Bywater*. Built at Milton in Cumbria in the 1860s, she was bought in 1921 by an Annalong syndicate and captained by William McKibbin until his retiral in 1925. She was used in the 1950 film *The Elusive Pimpernel*, which starred David Niven, Margaret Leighton and Cyril Cusack.

The letter 'K' on the funnel identifies this boat, moored at the quay in the 1920s, as having belonged to the fleet of John Kelly of Belfast. Shipping coal out of Garston on the Mersey, Kelly's 400–500 ton boats were unloaded by a gang of eight men who filled a one ton bucket, which was then hoisted by crane onto the quay and into wagons. Over winters throughout the 1920s, Warrenpoint took one delivery of coal per week.

The South Quay, viewed from 'Moffit's Corner' with the tram lines sweeping round from Marine Parade as they make their way to the railway station by the North Quay.

Havelock Place, looking back to Marine Parade with McCaughey's 'Noah's Ark' souvenir shop on the corner of Great George Street South. Built opposite the wooden pier in the nineteenth century as a customs' house, it was, by the 1930s, a Mecca for daytrippers.

The Café Royal on Marine Parade, photographed around 1910 when it was run by Hourican & Sons who had taken over from the Lawlor family two or three years before. Coming to Warrenpoint in a donkey and cart around 1903, the Houricans' first premises were in Duke Street before they took on the Marine Parade business. In the centre of the picture is Beach Cottage, on the Thomas Street corner, at that time the premises of Magee's Refreshment Rooms with McNally's Belfast Bar, later the Bee, attached at its side. Although its age cannot actually be ascertained, the cottage was reputedly the oldest house in the 'point until it was demolished in 2002 to make way for the building of Bay View Apartments. Beyond Thomas Street the terrace runs up to what was the Royal Hotel.

The Great Northern Hotel on the corner of Prince's Street and the Promenade in 1911. Built in two stages, the original part on the right was put up by H.R. Stanley in 1884 as the Beach Hotel, whilst the taller, grander, half to the left was built by the Great Northern Railway. Taking an interest in accommodation for their holiday-making passengers, in 1899 the Railway bought a hotel at Bundoran on Donegal Bay, this one in Warrenpoint and the Mourne and Woodside hotels at Rostrevor – and spent £50,000 upgrading them. The Woodside was sold shortly afterwards and in 1922 the Warrenpoint hotel was sold to the Sisters of Mercy for use as a school, which opened the following year as Our Lady of Lourdes Boarding School. The school moved out in 1930 and in 1938 the premises became St Joseph's Home for elderly men. Women were admitted from 1985 and it continues to serve this purpose today.

Built in the grounds of the Great Northern Hotel in 1906, the Pavilion served as a dance hall, entertainment centre and tearoom. The *Newry Reporter* of 27 July 1918 gave the Pavilion's programme for the following week: 'The Dublin Musical Players – a specially selected concert party, including Eileen Murnaghan (soprano), Agnes Sherry (mezzo soprano), Carlo Berckmans (the great tenor), Patrick Delaney (the celebrated Irish violinist) and Stan Wright (the inimitable humourist), in a programme changing nightly.' There were also 'special cinema films!', price of admission for which was 2/4d, 1/3d and a limited number at 8d, 'tax included'. When the hotel was bought by the Sisters of Mercy in 1922, the Pavilion became a classroom. The Sisters moved back to Newry, but the Pavilion continued as a National School until 2000. It now stands derelict in a sea of weeds.

A party of pierrots (entertainers led by a white-faced clown in loose, long-sleeved garb) perform on the temporary stage on the Promenade at the Osborne Prom corner in 1927. The group in this picture are unknown, but this 'traditional' entertainment started in Warrenpoint in 1906 when the Town Council's Amusements Committee invited the pierrots Adele and Sutton from Rhyl to play two performances per day for the season. The photograph comes from a postcard sent to Mrs Pryor of Prince Edward Road, Lewes, Sussex, with the message: 'Everybody backed Trigo [winner of the 1929 Derby]. Wish I'd come a few days earlier. His owner [W. Barnett of Cloghran Stud, near Dublin] crossed in our boat. Norman.'

Havelock Place in the 1920s with ferry passengers coming and going on the strand, with others, by the wall, just watching or waiting. Behind the centre pole, and set back between the lion topped ornate crow step gables, was the Royal Hotel building, by this time home to the Sisters of Mercy and now home to the Irish National Foresters, a benevolent society.

Beached ferry boats at Havelock Place on a quiet summer's morning in 1924. The popularity of this service to Omeath, particularly over the summer, is shown by the list of fifteen boatmen, including Thomas Cole, James McGeown and Francis Smith, in the 1913 Post Office Directory.

Peggy Boyle posing on a ferryboat on the Omeath side of Carlingford Lough in the summer of 1938. From 1870, Peggy's family owned Ma Boyle's Oyster Bar in Liverpool's Old Hall Street (this has been at Tower Gardens since June 1974). For many years Peggy was a regular summer visitor to Warrenpoint – as were some local lads to the Oyster Bar.

The Esplanade, with the swimming pool on the right and a jaunting car awaiting hire. The bay curves round to Rostrevor.

Sea View, stretching along the esplanade from the swimming pool entrance, in the 1930s. By this time, the tramway lines had long gone and the motor car and lorry had largely displaced the jaunting car and the cart.

Great George Street South, or, as it was in this early twentieth century photograph, Lower George Street. Stretching from the Shelbourne Tea Rooms to Osborne Prom, with the hills of County Louth beyond, it is pictured from the Church Street junction. The Recreation Ground is to the left. In the latter part of the nineteenth century Frank and Mary Carville's stables and jaunting-car hire business stood on the corner and about 1912 this three-storey building, which would later house the Alexandra Dance Hall, was erected. The dance hall was a popular venue until its closure in the 1950s and the building has now been converted into housing.

The Recreation Ground in the 1920s, looking north to Great George Street South and the spire of St Peter's Church. The trees and shrubs have since grown and matured and as the gardener could have told you – the grass just kept growing! In 1985 and 1993, Newry and Mourne District Council won the 'Ulster in Bloom' award for this 'outstandingly well kept Municipal Park'. St Peter's was built between 1836 and 1840, on land bequeathed by Sir George Ogle Godfrey of Newry. It was designed by the Newry architect Thomas Duff and built at a cost of £2,500. The spire was added in 1875.

The terrace of houses in Queen Street, looking onto the recreation ground, runs from the Promenade to the Great George Street junction and the Belfast Banking Co.'s three-storey red sandstone building at the far end. It is now the Northern Bank.

Warrenpoint (roller) Skating Rink, photographed at its opening on Wednesday, 1 June 1910, by which time there were over 570 in Britain. The rink at Rostrevor, burnt down seven years earlier, had opened in May 1877. Built by Messrs T. Anderson of Lagan Works, Belfast, to a design by the Coleraine architect J.S. Kennedy, the two hundred by sixty foot rink stood in what is now Great George Street North. For its opening night, the Great Northern Railway ran special cheap fare trains from as far off as Belfast. According to the *Newry Reporter*, 'striking as was the scene in the rink during daylight, it was nothing when the bright rays of electricity took its place. Coloured lights in hundreds, blended together, gave the rink a charmed appearance, and these changing to the powerful arc lights gave effects that were worth seeing'. The popularity of the rink, which also hosted dances and concerts, continued, but by the summer of 1918, Warrenpoint Amusements Ltd (having at some point bought out Messrs Kennedy & Co.) were in financial difficulties and closure was precipitated within days. The *Newry Reporter* of Thursday, 1 August 1918, brought news of Warrenpoint Hockey Club beating Newry 4–0, and, on the Saturday, news that the building, minus its fittings, had been sold at public auction, on 2 August 1918, to Messrs Ruddell, Harvey & Co. of Belfast for £3,000. The dynamo, engine, organ and other fittings were sold at auction as individual lots and the building was subsequently demolished.

Warrenpoint Golf Club's clubhouse in 1917. Inaugurated at a public meeting on 16 February 1893, under the captaincy of John J.F. Greene, the club's fifty-six members played over a six, later increased to nine, hole course on the lands at Dromore Villa. In November 1897, with backing from the Great Northern Railway (guests at their hotel would have free use of the course), the club moved to its present course on the adjacent lands of Captain Roger Hall, then president. The original clubhouse, Rose Cottage, was by then inadequate and plans for this new clubhouse were prepared by S. Wilson Reside and the contract for the £640 building awarded to Carvill & Sons of Warrenpoint. Officially opened on Easter Monday, 13 April 1914, the seventy by fifty foot building, with its verandah, held a club room, gentlemen's smoke room, ladies sitting room, and a council room. The caretaker's residence was in the roofspace. By the following year, 1915, there were 232 members (131 gentlemen and 101 ladies) and 900 visitors. One year short of its fiftieth anniversary, this clubhouse was destroyed by fire in February 1963. The present clubhouse, which replaced it, was opened on 24 September 1966.

Narrow Water Castle from the slipway on the south bank of the Newry River in County Louth, around 1940, with Charlie the ferryman resting on his oars awaiting his next hire. He charged 2d for a passenger and 1d for a bicycle. A mile up river from Carlingford Lough, the three-storey castle, or keep, and bawn were built around 1663 to defend the river approach to Newry. An earlier keep, built by Hugh de Lacy around 1212, was destroyed in the 1641 Rebellion.

In the days before its dedicated car parking areas, keep left bollards and safety railings, Rostrevor Square, as seen here in the early twentieth century, had an air of spaciousness. M'Brien's Crystal Hotel on the Bridge Street corner is now the Corner House Bar. The spire on the hill, breaking the skyline, belongs to St Mary's Star of the Sea Chapel, which was built around 1850 to replace the original build of 1744.

By the summer of 1920, when this photograph was taken, Patrick Morgan had taken over the Central Hotel from Arthur Hughes (see back cover caption), and school was out! On the left is the Church of Ireland's Kilbroney Parish Church, built in 1821 at a cost of £1837.4/- to accommodate a congregation of 350. The bulk of this money, £1,100, came as a loan from the Board of First Fruits (with a gift of £200) whilst the remainder was raised by subscription.

Early morning Bridge Street (previously Post Office Street) in the 1920s, with Patrick Morgan's Central Hotel on the left corner and Miss Catherine Brady's Cloughmore Hotel on the right. With six grocers in Bridge Street – Cole, Crawford, Irwin, Kaye, Murphy and Sinton – it was a busy area for the delivery vans of Inglis, the Belfast baker. Inglis' fleet of vans across the province were supplied each morning from Belfast by rail.

Flowing out of the Fairy Glen, the Rostrevor river passes Back Lane (now Water Street) and under the eighteenth century three-arched unhewn stone bridge which carries the road to Kilkeel. On 14 January 1938 the white two-storey house to the left became the Royal Ulster Constabulary barracks, with a complement of one sergeant, four constables, and three special constables. The sergeant, one constable and one special constable lived in the barracks. Sergeant E.J. Slavin was the last officer in charge when they closed on 16 April 1964.

The river above the road bridge, with Back Lane on the left, pictured in the summer of 1934. The Fairy Glen pathway is on the right, while Ivy Cottage is to the left.

Two cyclists make their way up Church Street, towards the Hilltown Road, in the early 1930s. But if they are off and pushing at this stage, Hilltown was a long walk! On the left is a gate pillar of St Mary's Star of the Sea Chapel, with the parochial house and St Mary's School on the right, and the tower of Kilbroney Parish Church against the distant hills of County Louth.

On the junction of Warrenpoint Road and New Road (now Shore Road) is a Mourne Mountains Touring Company bus. Founded in June 1913 by G.B. Morgan of the Mourne Hotel, the company ran mountain tours for hotel guests. Beyond the white house on Shore Road corner stands Rostrevor Presbyterian Church. From the 1840s, a growing Presbyterian congregation had met in Rostrevor's Dispensary in Mary Street, until in 1850, under the influence of the Rev. Thomas Smith Morgan, late of Fisherwick in Co. Antrim, funds from Belfast, Dublin and Liverpool allowed the purchase of the ground (£150) and the building of the church. Due to erosion, the twin pinnacles were removed in the 1950s.

Dominating the centre of this 1920s photograph is the Queen Victoria Home of the Girls' Friendly Society in Ireland. Coming to Warrenpoint in 1889, the Society transferred to rented premises at Rostrevor in 1893, before moving into this newly built home, which, with Royal permission, they named Queen Victoria Home in 1901. It was 'a Home of Rest for sick and weary Members' – although 'no one [could] be admitted who is recovering from any infectious illness, or who is in such weak health as to require special nursing'. After the Second World War it closed to become Mrs Thompson's Glencairn Guest House. She died in the late 1970s and, abandoned, it became derelict until purchased by the present owner in 1997. Removing the mature trees growing out of the ground floor windows was the first task in its renovation. Now known as Victoria House, it is a private dwelling.

Rostrevor Quay with the Mourne Hotel and the Woodside Hotel, with the Woodside Temperance Refreshments Rooms (for a time run by the auctioneer Bernard Dunn) between. Little is known of the Woodside, but the Mourne Hotel was built around 1870 by the public transport company, Norton of Belfast, on the site of the Quay Hotel. In 1899 both hotels were bought by the Great Northern Railway (with the Beach Hotel in Warrenpoint and another at Bundoran), although the Woodside was re-sold shortly afterwards. The Railway also took a controlling interest in the tramway. The Post Office Directory of 1913 describes the Mourne Hotel, or, as it then was, The Great Northern Hotel, as: '. . . surrounded by its own ornamental grounds, flower gardens and lawns, and [commanding] views of Carlingford Lough and the mountains on the other side.'

A Mourne Mountains Touring Company's thirteen-seater Dennis charabanc, with liveried driver, setting off for the day with a party of guests from the Mourne Hotel. Founded in 1907 by G.B. Morgan, manager of the hotel, the company had three charabancs and a number of buses to convey guests to and from Warrenpoint railway station.

Opened on 1 August 1877, to serve the newly opened Mourne Hotel, the Warrenpoint & Rostrevor Tramways Company's two foot ten inch gauge horse-drawn tramway ran from Warrenpoint railway station to the Mourne Hotel, with a short spur to Rostrevor Quay laid a few months later. Their rolling stock consisted of ten 'toast-racks', including the one shown here, and three single-deck saloons. The service ended in February 1915 when a storm washed away part of the track. Opposite J.C. Campbell's car showroom, at the gateway to the pier, the rounded corrugated roofed tram shed and stable survive, with a few yards of the track in granite setts.

Shore Road in 1924, with a schooner at the quay and the road towards the Woodside Hotel and Mourne Hotel busy with jaunting cars, motor cars and tourists.

According to the *Ordnance Survey Memoirs*, Rostrevor's 175 foot quay was built at the expense of John Martin of Kilbronie in 1745 for the landing of coal, two or three times a year, principally from Whitehaven in Cumberland, and for the convenience of coastguard boats. By the early twentieth century, Charles Sloan of Bridge Street was selling English and Scottish coal at 'moderate prices'. Later, these 'coal boats' carried away holly and oak for shipbuilding, and granite paviors. The last consignment of paviors was used on Liverpool's Lime Street. Today, the quay serves boats harvesting mussels during the season.

All traces of Cloughmore Tea Gardens were swept away when the entrance to Kilbroney Park moved from opposite the quay to its present position a few hundred yards north. The elderly gentleman to the left, who owned the tea room, is Mr Bernard J. Dunn, auctioneer and valuer, and grandfather of the founder of Dunn's Stores. To the left is the wall of Rostrevor's skating rink, opened in May 1877 and burnt down in December 1903.

Whether you believe the thirty ton granite Cloughmore Stone on Slieve Meen to be a glacial erratic, brought from Scotland in the Ice Age of 18,000 years ago, or a pebble placed there by the legendary Irish giant Finn McCool, it has been a curiosity for generations. Amongst the myriad of names and initials carved or chipped into its surface, the two most distinctive, and cut by the same hand, are, 'J. Glover, ME, Edinburgh (1850)' and 'H. Fulton, ME, Belfast'. The initials indicate them to have been mechanical engineers, but although the British Institute of Mechanical Engineers was founded in 1847, neither of them appear on its roll. This Edwardian mother and her family would have made the climb from some way below the position of the present car park!

Rostrevor House, the Ross Monument on the sweeping bend into the village, and Carlingford Lough, viewed from Thunders Hill in the 1930s. As the *Ordnance Survey Memoir* of Rostrevor, in the Parish of Kilbroney, was being written in 1836, Mrs Ross, the widow of the late Major General Robert Ross, was having the old Carrickbawn 'topsy-turvy' house, built by Mr Maguire, demolished, and the new house, shown in this photograph, built. Still informally known as 'topsy-turvy', the house is now home to the Convent of Our Lady of Apostles and Benedictine Monks. Erected in 1826 at a cost of £2,000, the grey, Mullaglass Quarry granite obelisk was designed by Henry Hamilton of Carpenham and celebrates the life of Major General Robert Ross of Bladensburgh, a hero of the American Campaign, who defeated the Americans at Bladensburg on 24 January 1814 and captured Washington. He was killed near Baltimore on 12 September 1814 and buried at St Paul's Church in Halifax, Nova Scotia.